Dedication

This book is dedicated to all our children. I know you have a fierce sense of what is right—to preserve what is precious in nature, to treat other people with kindness and respect.

Author's Note

This book was inspired by two of my trips to Costa Rica. In the first I called myself a "groupie," traveling along with the Oregon artists in this book when they visited the Costa Rican artists. While the artists sketched, I wrote.

Suddenly late in that trip, the inspiration one longs for happened. The simple sentence, we share a world, came to me. My concept was though we are so different in Oregon and Costa Rica, we both have tremendous natural beauty: the Pacific, large rivers, dense stands of trees, volcanoes...

I later spent three months in Costa Rica during the Trayvon Martin case coverage on tv that was highlighting the tragic shootings of young black men and feelings of injustice and estrangement in the black community. I kept thinking, How can this be? These are all our children. I then realized there must be two key messages to this book: We share a single world, not just through nature, but also in human relations.

Because the book grew out of the artist exchange, I asked each participating artist about collaborating. Every single one said yes. It would be hard to describe the delight I felt as their gorgeous submissions came to me. The best email attachments I ever received!

"Imagine all the people sharing all the world…"
John Lennon

"Imagínense toda la gente compartiendo todo el mundo…"
John Lennon

We share our world...

Compartimos el mundo...

"Live long, Mother Earth."
Indigenous People of the Andes

"Jallalla Pachamama."
Pueblo indígena andino

...Our planet Earth...

....Nuestro planeta La Tierra...

"One way to open your eyes is to ask yourself, 'What if I had never seen this before? What if I knew I would never see it again?'"
Rachel Carson

"Una manera de abrir los ojos es hacerse la pregunta, '¿Y si yo nunca hubiera visto esto antes? ¿Y si yo supiera que nunca volvería a verlo de nuevo?'"
Rachel Carson

...Suns, moons and stars...

...Soles, lunas y estrellas...

"...we have salt in our blood, in our sweat, in our tears. We are tied to the ocean."
John F. Kennedy

"...tenemos sal en la sangre, en el sudor, en las lágrimas. Tenemos un lazo con el mar."
John F. Kennedy

...Mysterious rolling oceans...

...Océanos ondulantes misteriosos...

"…my poetry was born between the hill and the river and took its voice from the rain…"
Pablo Neruda

"Mi poesía nació entre el cerro y el río y tomó su voz de la lluvia…"
Pablo Neruda

...Rivers, creeks and streams...

...Ríos, riachuelos y arroyos...

"Nature is resilient. If we give it a chance, it can and does come back. But we are moving so rapidly that we are not giving nature a chance."
Maya Lin

"La naturaleza se recupera. Si le damos la oportunidad, puede hacerlo y sí se recupera. Pero nos movemos a tal velocidad que no le damos esa posibilidad a la naturaleza."
Maya Lin

...Wetlands, mangrove swamps, marshes and bogs...

...Humedales, manglares, pantanos y ciénagas...

"…He's allowed me to go up to the mountain…. I've seen the Promised Land. I may not get there with you. But…we, as a people, will get to the Promised Land."
Dr. Martin Luther King Jr.

"…Él me ha permitido subir a la montaña…. He visto la Tierra Prometida. Puede que no llegue con ustedes. Pero…nosotros, como pueblo, llegaremos a la Tierra Prometida."
Dr. Martin Luther King Jr.

...Mountains, some quiet and some on fire...

...Montañas, algunas tranquilas, otras en llamas...

"I went to the woods because I wished to live deliberately, to front only the essential facts of life and see if I could not learn what it had to teach…"
Henry David Thoreau

"Fui al bosque porque deseaba vivir deliberadamente, para convivir solamente con los hechos fundamentales de la vida y para ver si podía o no aprender lo que tenía que enseñarme…"
Henry David Thoreau

...Forests filled with green,
then more green...

...Bosques llenos de verde,
entonces más verde...

"I paint flowers so they will not die."
Frida Kahlo

"Pinto flores para que no se mueran."
Frida Kahlo

...Trees, plants and flowers...

...Árboles, plantas y flores...

"When we try to pick out anything by itself, we find it hitched
to everything else in the universe."
John Muir

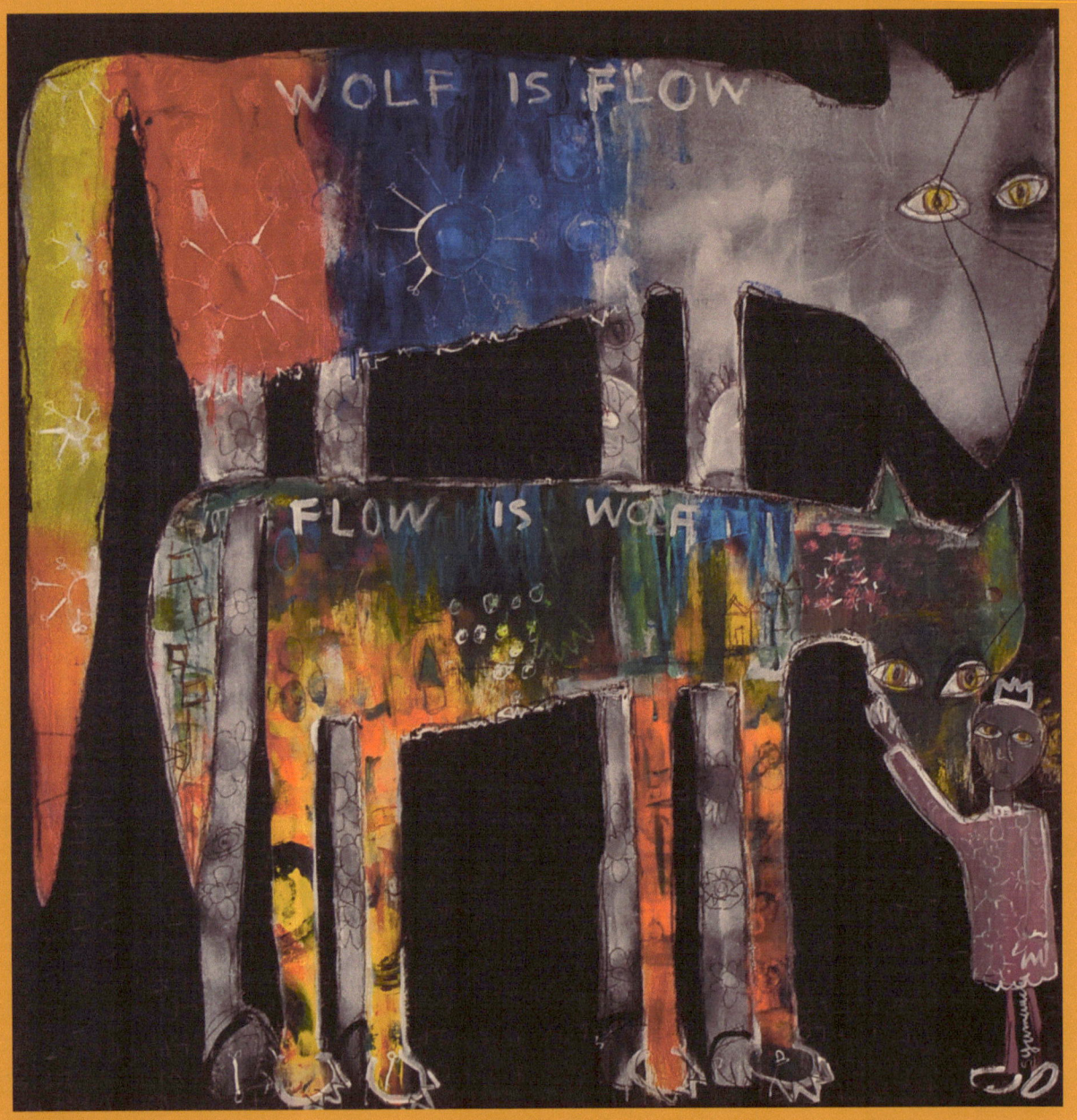

"Cuando intentamos apartar algo, descubrimos que está amarrado
a todo lo demás en el universo."
John Muir

...Animals on the land...

...Animales en la tierra...

"The sea, once it casts its spell, holds one in its net of wonder forever."
Jacques Cousteau

"El mar, una vez que nos hechiza, nos cautiva en su red asombrosa para siempre."
Jacques Cousteau

...Animals living in the seas...

...Animales que viven en los mares...

"I know why the caged bird sings."
Maya Angelou

"Yo sé por qué canta el pájaro enjaulado."
Maya Angelou

...Birds at home on the air...

...Pájaros a gusto en el aire...

"Human beings are not always born forever on the day that their mothers give birth to them. Rather life forces them to give birth to themselves time and again."
Gabriel García Márquez

"Los seres humanos no nacen para siempre el día en que sus madres los alumbran sino que la vida los obliga a parirse a sí mismos una y otra vez."
Gabriel García Márquez

...Plus winged butterflies and bees...

...Además, mariposas y abejas con alas...

"….we need more love in the world…more kindness, more compassion, more joy, more laughter."
Ellen DeGeneres

"…necesitamos más amor en el mundo. . .más bondad, más compasión, más alegría, más risa."
Ellen de Generes

...Every beautiful creature,
including us!

...Cada criatura hermosa,
incluso nosotros!

"Man needs music, literature and painting…to compensate
for the rudeness and materialism of life."
Fernando Botero

"El hombre necesita la música, la literatura y la pintura…para compensar
por la tosquedad y el materialismo de la vida."
Fernando Botero

Artist Statements

The artists in this book participated in an Oregon–Costa Rica art/culture exchange through Partners of the Americas.

When the Costa Rican artists visited Oregon in 2010, Partners welcomed them with three shows to highlight their art. Their hosts shared picnicking, hiking, kayaking in mountain lakes, a trip to the beach, a 4th of July parade and rodeo, and visits to artists' studios and galleries.

The Oregon artists' 2012 visit to Costa Rica started with attendance at San Jose's Festival de las Artes, the international festival of art and music. The artists met daily to paint, draw, and sculpt. They also visited galleries and artists' studios, sketched in scenic landscapes, and co-sponsored a show of the Oregon and Costa Rican artists.

The artists continue to exchange their love of visual arts and their respect for each other by collaborating on this book.

Sonia Alfaro Alfaro es costarricense, es bachiller en Estudios Sociales, en Artes Plásticas con énfasis en Pintura y en Enseñanza de las Artes Plásticas por la Universidad de Costa Rica. Ha expuesto de forma individual y colectiva en importantes espacios a nivel nacional, también ha expuesto sus obras en Francia, Estados Unidos, España, Grecia y México. Ha trabajado como docente para el Ministerio de Educación Pública de Costa Rica. Contacto: soniaalfaro13@hotmail.com
                                                                                    Sonia Alfaro Alfaro

What do I want to remember? How red and orange blossoms complement both a green Oregon field and the blue sky and sea of Costa Rica. My lifetime as an artist has led me to gratefully share these moments in this book.   Jan Aungier

Las imágenes que pinto se manifiestan en momentos de paz e inspiración. Unas líneas me llevan a otras y con el uso de colores brillantes y del negro, se va formando la historia pintada. En cada una de mis pinturas hay una historia. ¡Encuéntrala! Facebook: Marisa Baragli's Art Page
                                                                                    Marisa Luisa Baragli

Esteban is a muralist with commissioned artwork in Costa Rica, the United States and Spain. He received his BFA in Painting with an emphasis in Public Art, from the Pacific Northwest College of Art. His subject matter is environmentally focused, bridging biology, education and fine art. Most of his artwork has been produced in public spaces where he works with community leaders during the design process and involves local youth in the painting and production. website: be.net/ecomurals

Esteban Camacho Steffensen

I studied Advertising Design at the College of Fine Arts at the Autonomous University of Central America in San José, Costa Rica, as well as painting and printmaking in studios of national artists. My work has transitioned from figurative realism to abstract expression, with the central theme of human experience. In watercolor, one of my favorite techniques is to explore any topic that allows me the freedom and spontaneity of the medium, such as imaginary landscapes, magic objects, and new worlds. www.facebook.com/MagdaCordobaArt

Magda Cordoba

Paige Gabriela-Lambert is an Oregon girl who loves adventure. I think it is my job as an artist to reflect the delights and despairs I experience in the people I meet around the world. The Pacific coast, Mt Hood and colorful festivals fill my summer days; and when it's cold, the Caribbean island of Utila is my home. My sketchbook is never far. I love to draw and I think that helps carry into my sculptures, some of the expression and feeling of the people I see in my travels.

Paige Gabriela-Lambert

The natural world of the High Desert in Central Oregon where I live is my inspiration. I draw, paint and carve wildflowers onto my pottery - Poppies, Lupine, Indian Paintbrushes, Sunflowers, Arrowleaf Balsamroot, Violets, Hedgehog Cactus, and Blue Flax. Beauty of the outdoors comes into the home through my art made for everyday use.
            Janet Matson

Bachiller en Artes Plásticas con énfasis en Pintura por la Universidad de Costa Rica, actualmente es estudiante de Sociología y de la Maestría en Comunicación y Desarrollo, además trabaja como ilustradora y diseñadora en el Programa Kioscos Socio-ambientales para la Organización Comunitaria, en la misma universidad. Es co-fundadora del colectivo Pintacuentos Diseño Artesanal y del Centro Cultural Caña Dulce, en Grecia, Alajuela, Costa Rica. Ha realizado proyectos en los que combina su pasión por la ilustración y la literatura con la investigación y la acción social, en temas relacionados con migración, género y ciudadanías. www.behance.net/quelmoravega   Raquel Mora Vega

Photography is one way that Chuck Steury of Portland, Oregon stays truly mindful. He discovers beauty, in things both large and small, in each setting and moment he and his camera find themselves. Share these images and moments with him at Chuck Steury Photography on Facebook.   Chuck Steury

Licenciada en Artes Plásticas con énfasis en Pintura de la Universidad de Costa Rica. Ha participado en más de 23 exposiciones colectivas a nivel nacional y 2 internacionales, 1 exposición individual, 6 ferias, Encuentro Centroamericano de Mujeres en las Artes, 8 concursos. Ha realizado 6 murales, uno ganador del primer lugar en el Certamen de Pintura Mural "Café, Tradición y Sostenibilidad." Ha laborado como profesora en colegios e impartido cursos en universidades. En el 2008 obtiene una Licenciatura en Educación con énfasis en Pintura en la UNED. artetrejos@yahoo.com   Jeannette Trejos Rodríguez

Artista costarricense graduada en la Universidad de Costa Rica, ha dedicado su vida a la pintura y, al mismo tiempo, a compartir sus conocimientos y amor por el arte con muchísimas generaciones de niñas y niños de su ciudad, desde su escuela de pintura. Su obra se caracteriza por la experimentación con diferentes texturas y la pasión por el color. Una de sus temáticas recurrentes es la figura humana y sobre todo la figura femenina, haciendo alusión a las mujeres fuertes que son parte de su historia, mujeres luchadoras, protectoras de la vida. Ha realizado exposiciones en Francia, Italia, Estados Unidos y en reconocidos espacios de su país.
                                                                                              Rose Mery Vega Zeledón

Samyak "Sam" Yamauchi is an intuitive, stream-of-consciousness painter and teacher in Portland, Oregon. A self-taught artist, her paintings can be found at art shows, galleries, and art festivals around the region. A believer in personal evolution as a means to support the planet, Sam's paintings hold the joy and power of creative inspiration. Her website is samyakyamauchi.com   Samyak Yamauchi

"…you, irrespective of your age, should place human solidarity, the concern for the other, at the center of the values by which you live."
Nelson Mandela

"Usted, sin importar su edad, debe enfocar los valores por los que usted vive en la solidaridad humana, o sea, el interés por el prójimo."
Nelson Mandela

Acknowledgments

This book is about sharing a single world. We are one in terms of our common humanity and the beautiful natural world embracing us. The book itself would not exist without a lot of people sharing with me: belief in me, careful listening, financial support, knowledge, creativity, research, opinions, fluency in both English and Spanish…

One person just tipped me off that a quote I loved had actually been discredited. A few simply pointed me in the direction of important thinking. Others were with me through emails and phone calls, meetings over coffee, lunch, and dinner--all the way from dream to book launch reality. Some I met once, yet they began to share immediately. Some have been sharing with me for years (including my best friend of over 50 years!).

Thank you to all these who helped, in particular: Karen Graham, Marilyn McDonald, Michele Stemler, Marjie Sandoz, Pat Schmuck, Marisa Baragli Bevington; the exchange artists—Jan, Paige, Pat, Sam, Marisa, Janet, Chuck, Esteban, Raquel, Rose Mery, Sonia, Magda and Jeanette; my family—Jenn, Dale, Aidan, Kaitlyn, Ava, and Linda; Elena Chavarría Correa, Elena García Velasco, Elena Valdés Chavarría, Elaine Newton-Bruzza; Don Ruff, Javier Thellaeche, Pedro Medina; folks who trust me to house/pet sit, giving me tranquil respite; baristas and servers at the cafes where I wrote on my laptop for hours; libraries where I also hang out, especially the Sterling Writer's Room in the historic Central library in Portland; wonderful children's book writers and illustrators, masters of few words, but big ideas and enchanting images; Luz Adriana Restrepo, Jorge Fabián González; Olga Sanchez of Milagro Theatre; Naysi Luis; book designer Cheryl McLean; Partners of the Americas; the Graham Family Foundation, Starseed Foundation; PNCA Arlene and Harold Schnitzer Center for Art and Design.

Agradecimientos

www.ingramcontent.com/pod-product-compliance
Lightning Source LLC
Chambersburg PA
CBHW042146290426
44110CB00002B/129